AF269453

FRANCE

R.L. Van

Big Buddy Books
An Imprint of Abdo Publishing
abdobooks.com

abdobooks.com

Published by Abdo Publishing, a division of ABDO, PO Box 398166, Minneapolis, Minnesota 55439.
Copyright © 2023 by Abdo Consulting Group, Inc. International copyrights reserved in all countries. No part of this book may be reproduced in any form without written permission from the publisher. Big Buddy Books™ is a trademark and logo of Abdo Publishing.

Printed in the United States of America, North Mankato, Minnesota
102022
012023

Design: Emily O'Malley, Mighty Media, Inc.
Production: Mighty Media, Inc.
Editor: Jessica Rusick
Cover Photograph: WDG Photo/Shutterstock Images
Interior Photographs: AP Images, p. 21; connel/Shutterstock Images, p. 13; Elena Pominova/Shutterstock Images, p. 19; Everett Collection/Shutterstock Images, p. 9; HAY Adrien/Shutterstock Images, p. 15; Influential Photography/Shutterstock Images, p. 23; larik_malasha/Shutterstock Images, p. 27 (top right); LiliGraphie/Shutterstock Images, p. 30 (currency); lukulo/iStockphoto, pp. 5 (compass), 7 (compass); Martin M303/Shutterstock Images, p. 25; Media Home/Shutterstock Images, p. 30 (flag); Nattee Chalermtiragool/Shutterstock Images, pp. 27 (top left), 28 (bottom); Pau Vives/Shutterstock Images, p. 26 (left); Pawel Kazmierczak/Shutterstock Images, p. 17; Pyty/Shutterstock Images, p. 5 (world map); Radu Razvan/Shutterstock Images, p. 29 (top); Robert Biedermann/Shutterstock Images, p. 7 (map); Samuel Borges Photography/Shutterstock Images, p. 6 (bottom); The U.S. Army/Flickr, p. 11; trabantos/Shutterstock Images, p. 6 (middle); V_E/Shutterstock Images, p. 27 (bottom); Whatafoto/Shutterstock Images, p. 6 (top); Wikimedia Commons, pp. 26 (right), 28 (top), 29 (bottom)
Design Elements: Mighty Media, Inc.
Country population and area figures taken from the CIA World Factbook

Library of Congress Control Number: 2022940511

Publisher's Cataloging-in-Publication Data
Names: Van, R.L., author.
Title: France / by R.L. Van
Description: Minneapolis, Minnesota : Abdo Publishing, 2023 | Series: Countries | Includes online resources and index.
Identifiers: ISBN 9781532199608 (lib. bdg.) | ISBN 9781098274801 (ebook)
Subjects: LCSH: France--Juvenile literature. | Europe--Juvenile literature. | France--History--Juvenile literature. | Geography--Juvenile literature.
Classification: DDC 944--dc23

CONTENTS

PASSPORT TO FRANCE

France is a country in western Europe. It also has many **territories** around the world. About 68 million people live in France and its territories.

WHERE IS FRANCE?
N
W E
S
United Kingdom
English Channel
Belgium
Germany
Luxembourg
FRANCE
Switzerland
Bay of Biscay
Italy
Andorra
Spain
Mediterranean Sea

IMPORTANT CITIES

Paris is France's **capital** and largest city. It is a center of business, culture, education, and politics.

Lyon has France's second-largest metropolitan area. It is known for its food and historical sites.

Marseille has France's third-largest metropolitan area. It is a major port city.

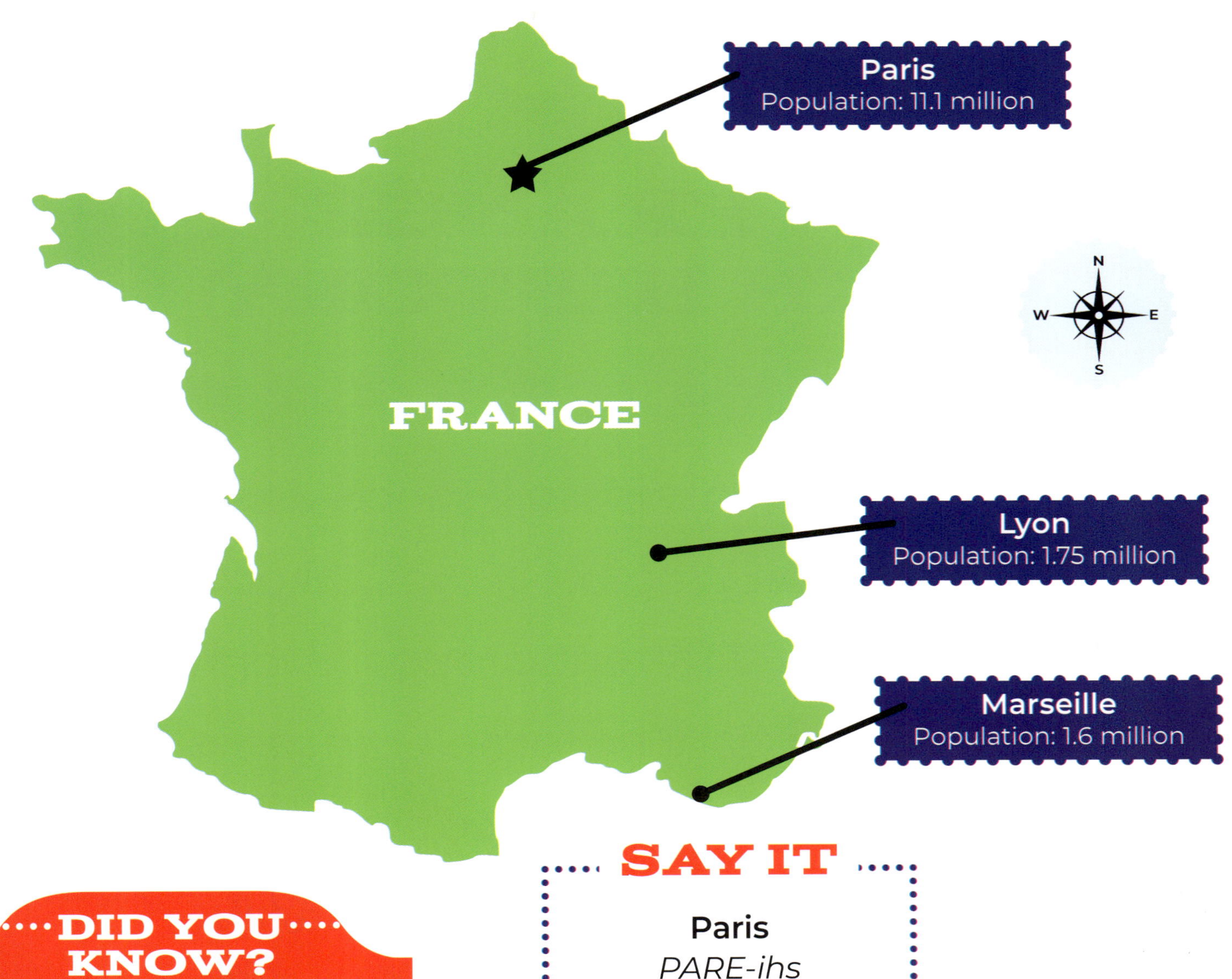

Paris
Population: 11.1 million

Lyon
Population: 1.75 million

Marseille
Population: 1.6 million

FRANCE

N
W   E
S

DID YOU KNOW?

Paris is known as the "City of Light."

SAY IT

Paris
PARE-ihs

Lyon
Lee-OHN

Marseille
mahr-SAY

FRANCE IN HISTORY

In ancient times, France was part of the Gaul region. It was taken over by many different groups. Eventually, western Gaul became France.

In the 1700s, France's people struggled. They wanted a say in government. They began the French **Revolution** in 1789.

Revolutionaries took France's king and queen as prisoners during the French Revolution.

After the French **Revolution**, France's government changed many times. For the most part, it has been a **republic** since 1870.

France struggled during **World War I** and **World War II**. Many people died. The wars used many of France's **resources**. But after World War II, the French began to rebuild.

American soldiers arrive in Normandy, France, on D-Day, June 6, 1944. This invasion marked a turning point in World War II.

AN IMPORTANT SYMBOL

France's flag is called the French Tricolor. It has blue, white, and red stripes.

France's government is a **semi-presidential republic**. The parliament makes laws. The president is head of state. The prime minister is head of government.

Blue and red are the traditional colors of Paris. White represents France's Bourbon monarchy.

ACROSS THE LAND

France has cliffs, forests, coasts, and rivers. It is home to the French Alps and the Pyrenees Mountains.

France's animals include chamois, Alpine marmots, and deer. Lavender, wildflowers, and many types of trees grow there.

SAY IT

Chamois
SHAM-ee

Chamois are hooved animals that eat grass, moss, and lichen.

EARNING A LIVING

France's factories make aircraft, cars, wine, and beauty products. Many French people work in health care jobs and banking.

France has important **resources**. Salt, stone, and gravel are mined there. Farmers produce grains, sugar beets, milk, beef, and wine.

French farmers harvest wine grapes from August to October.

DID YOU KNOW?

France is the world's biggest wine exporter.

LIFE IN FRANCE

Many famous writers and thinkers have come from France. France is also known for its cheeses, breads, and pastries. Wine is a popular drink.

The French enjoy cycling, soccer, tennis, and rugby. Many French people belong to the Roman Catholic Church.

France is famous for its *boulangeries*, or bakeries.

8

FAMOUS FACES

● ● ● ● ● ● ● ● ● ● ● ● ● ●

French dancer, singer, and actress Josephine Baker was born in the United States. She became a French citizen in 1937. Baker was the first Black woman to appear in a major motion picture. She was also a civil rights activist.

Josephine Baker continued performing until her death in 1975.

Professional soccer player Kylian Mbappé was born in Paris. He began playing for France's national league at age 16. In 2018, he helped the French national team win the World Cup. In 2020, he started a charity to help children.

Kylian Mbappé has his own
collection of sneakers sold
by sports company Nike.

9

A GREAT COUNTRY

France is known for its history and culture. The people and places of France help make the world a more interesting place.

Many French villages, including Saint-Cirq-Lapopie, were founded in medieval times.

If you ever visit France, here are some places to go and things to do!

PLAY

Try to snap a picture of an Alpine marmot at Vanoise National Park!

DISCOVER

Visit Grand Île in Strasbourg. Some say it looks like a fairy-tale town!

LEARN

Visit some of France's many museums, including the Louvre art museum.

EAT

Take a break at a sidewalk café with some *pain au chocolat* (chocolate croissants) or crêpes.

EXPLORE

See the Palace of Versailles during warm months to explore the beautiful gardens.

TIMELINE

1429

At about age 17, Joan of Arc led French soldiers to win an important battle against English soldiers in the Hundred Years' War.

1860s

French artists, including Monet, Degas, and Renoir, began painting in the **impressionist** style.

1793

The Louvre Museum opened as an art museum in Paris.

1919

The Treaty of Versailles was signed at France's Palace of Versailles, ending **World War** I.

2013

The 100th Tour de France cycling race took place.

1889

People saw the Eiffel Tower for the first time at a world's fair.

2018

France won its second World Cup title.

FRANCE
UP CLOSE

Official Name
French Republic

Flag

Population
68,305,148 (2022 est.)
21st-most-populated country

Total Area
248,573 square miles
(643,801 sq km)
44th-largest country

Official Language
French

Capital
Paris

Currency
Euro

Form of Government
Semi-presidential
republic

National Anthem
"La Marseillaise"
("The Song of
Marseille")

GLOSSARY

capital—a city where government leaders meet.

impressionist—a style of painting that focused on accurately showing light and color.

republic—a government in which the people choose the leader.

resource—a supply of something useful or valued.

revolution—the forced overthrow of a government for a new system.

semi-presidential republic—a form of government in which an elected president shares power with a prime minister and an elected legislature.

territories—areas that are not states but are under the authority of a country's government.

World War I—a war fought in Europe from 1914 to 1918.

World War II—a war fought in Europe, Asia, and Africa from 1939 to 1945.

ONLINE RESOURCES

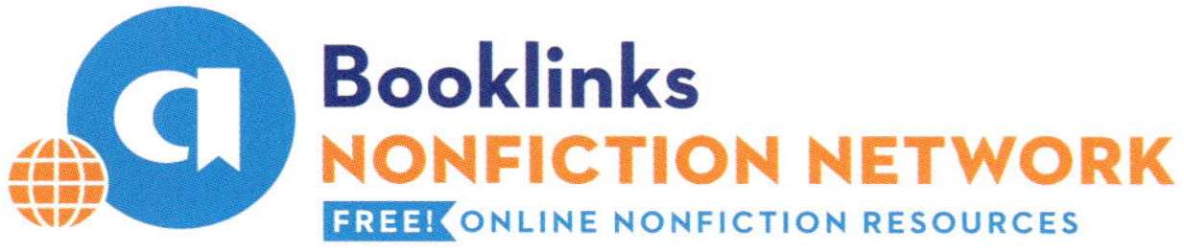

To learn more about France, please visit **abdobooklinks.com** or scan this QR code. These links are routinely monitored and updated to provide the most current information available.

INDEX